A CHRISTIAN PERSPECTIVE ON HOMOSEXUALITY

DANIEL W. PUL

Edited by Thomas J. Doyle
Cover photos: background, D. Jeanene Tiner; inset, H. Armstrong Roberts, Inc.

3558 S. Jefferson Avenue, St. Louis, MO 63118-3968
Manufactured in the United States of America

CONTENTS

PREFACE

ABOUT THE CHRISTIAN PERSPECTIVE SERIES

How often haven't we been confronted with an issue that challenges us? It nags at our patience, frustrating us in our desire to honor God in the way we handle, manage, and react to the issue in our daily lives. We struggle, unable to find the right approach or perspective. Some issues may even cause us to question God and His power and presence in our lives. At times we may feel helpless and weak in the way we react to an issue—baby Christians wondering if we will ever grow up. Feeling unworthy and ill-equipped to be the witnesses of Jesus in an unreceptive or apathetic world, we may echo the sentiments of Agur of old, who marveled at the greatness of God in comparison with his own inadequacies. He said,

> I am the most ignorant of men; I do not have a man's understanding. I have not learned wisdom, nor have I knowledge of the Holy One. Who has gone up to heaven and come down? Who has gathered up the wind in the hollow of his hands? Who has wrapped up the waters in his cloak? Who has established all the ends of the earth? What is his name, and the name of his son? Tell me if you know! (Proverbs 30:2–4)

Fortunately, God didn't leave us alone to struggle with those things that challenge us and cause us to pause when we don't know what to think or how to respond. With a love for us that reaches back before the beginning of time and connects us with a crude wooden cross that stood in Palestine some 2,000 years ago, God cares about our everyday concerns. He has given us the direction, counsel, and forgiveness of His holy Word to help us live lives in joyful response to all that He has done for us through Jesus, His Son and our Savior.

Each title in the Christian Perspective series has been designed to provide the insights and reflections of an author who has personally confronted an issue that touches us and challenges our lives of faith in one way or another. He or she has sought the counsel and application of God's holy Word to this topic and has put his or her thoughts and conclusions in writing to give others confronted with the same issue a "jump start" in their thinking.

The Christian Perspective series has been designed in the book-study format, organized in chapters and suitable for either individual use or group study. You may choose to write notes in the margins as you read. Following the reading of each chapter, questions have been provided to further stimulate your thinking and to serve as discussion starters if the book-study is being used in a small-group setting. May God bless you as you explore the topic of this course.

Suggestions for Using This Course in a Group Setting

Select a leader for the course or a leader for the day. It will be the leader's responsibility to keep the discussion moving and to help involve everyone.

Emphasize sharing. Your class will work best if the participants feel comfortable with one another and if all feel that their contributions to the class discussion are important and useful. Take the necessary time at the beginning of the course to get to know one another. You might share names, occupations, hobbies, etc. Share what you expect to gain from this course. Take some time at the beginning of each class session to allow participants to share experiences and news items from the week that relate to your study. Be open and accepting. Don't force anyone to speak. The course will be most helpful if participants willingly share deep feelings, problems, doubts, fears, and joys. That will require building an atmosphere of openness, trust, and caring about one another. Take time to build relationships among participants. That time will not be wasted!

Find ways to keep the session informal. Meet in casual surroundings. Arrange seating so participants can face one another. Ask volunteers to provide refreshments.

Depend on the Holy Spirit. Expect His presence. He will guide you and cause you to grow through the study of His holy Word. He has promised that His Word will not return empty (Isaiah 55:11). But do not expect the Spirit to do your work for you!

Start early! Prepare well! As time permits, do additional reading about the topic. Begin and end with prayer.

Begin and end on time. Punctuality is a courtesy to everyone and can be a factor that will encourage discussion.

Keep the class moving. Ask the leader to move the class along from section to section in the study guide. Limit your discussion to questions of interest to the participants. Be selective. You don't need to cover every question and every Bible verse.

Work to build up one another through your fellowship and study. You have your needs; other group members have theirs. Together you have a lot to gain.

Be sensitive to any participants who may have needs related to the specific topics discussed in this course.

Be a "gatekeeper." That means you may need to shut the gate of conversation on one person while you open it for someone else. Endeavor to involve everyone, especially those who hesitate to speak.

Expect and rejoice in God's presence and blessing as He builds your faith and enriches your life.

INTRODUCTION

This short book will not provide you with all the answers about homosexuality. However, I hope that what I write will encourage you to think about, pray for, and develop a Christlike heart toward the person struggling with homosexuality. God has clearly indicated in His Word what He intends for healthy sexual expression. Therefore, how Christians respond to the homosexual is important, and I will attempt to speak to this sensitive issue. My desire is that you be challenged as well as built up in God's Word through the insights and knowledge presented.

Today we hear a great deal about homosexuality, and we are forced to think about issues that were not a concern to most people a decade ago—certainly not within the church. Yet I believe that many people do not have a clear understanding of the person with homosexual desires. And with little understanding, many people fear the issue—which can lead to anger, hatred, and prejudice. At the very least, the fear encourages people to avoid discussing the topic altogether. While these defenses protect us, they also bar us from gaining a deeper understanding of what it is all about and how the Lord wants us to respond to the homosexual.

Knowledge alone is not going to change hearts and attitudes. Yes, God has revealed through His Word truths about Himself and the nature of man. However, He does not simply implant it in us through a kind of robotic programming. Rather through the ongoing work of the Holy Spirit, His Word continually becomes a real part of us. And that takes time. God allows us to grow through our experiences and the challenges that confront us as we apply His Word to and in our lives.

As you read this book, you may feel a tension between wanting to enforce God's Law and yet to offer the sweet Gospel of God's love in Christ Jesus for all. Good. Such a tension can foster growth. It can encourage a tender heart of compassion as well as strengthen your value of sexuality for men and women as God intended.

If you are looking for examples of heinous acts committed by some homosexuals, of ammunition to blast the homosexual lifestyle, you will not find it here. Such activity does occur; however, some homosexuals do not engage in such acts—or in any sexual behavior at all. This book will not focus on acts but on the homosexual *person* and how God has chosen to deal with this concern.

Our media today depict homosexuals and the homosexual lifestyle in a variety of ways. There are portraits of positive, functioning homosexual couples, portraits that paint the lifestyle as a legitimate alternative. There are also the pictures of hostile, angry, militant homosexuals—portraits that often fuel the fire of animosity between them and those they oppose.

There is, however, a whole other realm of individuals who are seldom heard of and rarely known. They are the ones who go to church with you. They have been with you in Sunday school. Sometimes they are full-time church workers or leaders. They are Christians who love and know Jesus as their Savior. They struggle in silence, often because they do not understand these feelings they have—and they know it's easier to keep quiet than to face the fear and the shame of being known. Some homosexuals have left the church in order to fulfill the longings and desires they have felt since they can remember. Others the Lord has touched and called out of hurtful, painful, and abusive situations that have included homosexual activity. But they all have at least this in common: they need the love, care, and support of brothers and sisters in the church that comes only from our forgiving Savior.

It is for the person who struggles in silence that I write.

This book is also a good place to start for the person who wants to begin understanding the friend or Christian brother or sister who has homosexual desires. It is my hope to engage your heart and your mind into the midst of their struggle. As your understanding is increased, I pray that your heart is opened as well. God wants you to have the hope for healing and transformation as well as the compassion to love as He loves.

1

My Journey

> Praise be to the God and Father of our Lord Jesus Christ, the Father of compassion and the God of all comfort, who comforts us in all our troubles, so that we can comfort those in any trouble with the comfort we ourselves have received from God. (2 Corinthians 1:3–4)

I begin with my own story. It is a testimony unique to me—a point I need to stress. Each person who has had homosexual feelings has his or her own experiences and has reacted in his or her own unique way. Still, that said, my story is not unlike many others. It is a message that God does enter and work in the deepest and darkest places of our hearts and lives.

My feelings of guilt and shame in my struggle with sexuality were extremely painful and difficult. I remember reciting in my head, "How could you have these desires? No other Christians have them." I questioned my faith. I questioned God. I simply could not understand or experience God's grace and love in this part of my life.

I felt very alone. Raised in a pastor's home, I felt I did not have a place to go. It was too risky to share with another pastor or teacher, and I did not know how to begin to talk with my dad about it. I was afraid—frightened of rejection. I felt I needed to protect an image that other people had of me: a good Christian and a good boy. It was easier to carry on as if everything was normal than to risk sharing. So I chose not to allow anyone else to know this part of me.

I did not know where the feelings and desires came from. I recall wondering early in life about some of the longings that I had, but it was not until around age 11 or so that the feelings began to take on an erotic nature and I found myself having homosexual fantasies and thoughts. I would often entertain them, but then the feelings of self-hatred and guilt would come. And so a cycle of conflicting desires emerged.

What guilt I felt because my desires were homosexual! My shame became a thick wall that no one could penetrate. But I was split in two. I portrayed myself as a good student, a caring friend, a nice son—and yet continued to take part in the self-pleasuring sexual behavior. So I spun from sin to guilt to the mask of respectability to sin to guilt and round and round.

This ride from hell got worse as I paired my ongoing behavior with pornography. My secret acts not only perpetuated the cycle but made it worse. I could never talk about the pornography. What had been a problem inside had now produced tangible evidence that I hated. Thus the wall of shame and guilt grew higher and stronger, and I knew I could never open up to talk with anybody about my true self.

At the same time, however, I knew God was not unaware of my sin. My heart's cry was to have the desires and the drives go away. How many times I prayed for God to remove them! I wanted God to change me and somehow, miraculously, just take away the urges and the drives.

I loathed the part of me that was drawn toward fantasy and pornography. I thought, if only I could get rid of this "little part" of my life, I would be okay. If I could just stop my behavior, then at least I would not have the shame and guilt and I could at last be at peace with myself and with God.

I found I could control my behavior for a few weeks or months. Eventually, however, I would succumb. I would be feeling good about my walk with the Lord and the shame would be gone; but when I fell, it would always come back in its full strength and then some. Even though I knew Jesus died for my sin and had forgiven me, I could not feel His presence in the midst of my shame. An intimate and consistent relationship with the Lord seemed impossible.

In some ways, life was good. While I was in high school, I was active in my congregation's youth group. I genuinely enjoyed the friends I had and the fellowship we shared. I know now that there were ways I was maturing in my faith as I continuously participated in Bible studies as well as in worship.

My family also was important to me. I cared a great deal for my parents and three brothers. We enjoyed meal time, having devotions, and going on family vacations together. I attended a Lutheran grade school along with my brothers. I still treasure the values I learned through my family and the school experiences I had as a boy. I appreciate the love and care of my family, my church, and my friends.

Yet my nearly ideal life made my conflict even more difficult. If anyone ever were to know what was inside of me, I would not be able to bear it. I had to remain silent. I knew what people thought of homosexuals. Hearing the jokes at school, teasing with brothers and friends, and of course knowing what the Bible said about homosexuality ruled out any safe place to share. How could I begin to trust anyone with something that I felt was bigger than life? I knew I did not want to be gay, but I did not have another place to turn to.

Along with my three brothers, I had a fair number of male friends, and I did not have a problem with being shy. I have since come to understand, however, that there is something about the nature of the homosexual struggle that distorted the ways I related to them. Not feeling secure in my identity as a male, I did not perceive myself as adept at or even eligible for typical boys' activities. Though I participated in them to some degree, there was still a kind of emptiness. I never did feel like "one of the guys."

I felt more comfortable relating to female friends, and I hoped to experience more than just a friendship with a girl. I thought that might generate a new desire for females and replace any homosexual tendencies—that I'd finally be "normal." All I wanted was a normal boy-girl relationship, but I really did not know what it should be like.

Boys usually feel awkward when going out with a girl for the first time. But that's not what I sensed. I felt uneasy, trying to be something I was not. I felt fake. I was going through the motions of being the kind of person I thought I should be. I did not have the maturity to think about what I was doing to myself or to the girl with whom I was involved. But still, I could not risk telling her the truth about how I felt. And the desires I had hoped would develop never did. Dating left me empty, confirming the feelings that I was different.

Going away to a college different from the one both my older brothers attended was significant in a number of ways. The choice to establish "my own territory" helped me gain some independence, and it took me away from a lot of familiar patterns. I was making a fresh start, and I began to identify myself apart from my family and my church. New friends, new challenges, a new environment, and the exposure to a lot of new ideas forced me to test the values and spiritual truths in which I was raised and to make them my own. And I did. During this time I began to grow deeper and closer in my personal relationship to the Lord. My own identity was growing. My resolve not to allow pornography to have the place it once did grew stronger. And my lifestyle changed for the better. Looking back, I see that these were important changes. However, more needed to be done. The desires still haunted me, even though I pushed them down further and further.

At college, I met a very special young woman: Janine. Her kind and spirited personality really drew me, and we developed a deep friendship. I felt closer to her than almost anyone. She had many qualities I felt I would want in a wife if I were ever to marry.

Trying to initiate a romantic relationship with her was a step I took hesitatingly. Actually, I wasn't feeling a romantic attraction as much as a simple desire to know her more deeply. I felt that I could really care for someone like her, and my feelings did grow deeper and fonder. But with the presence of my underlying, conflicting homosexual desires, I also felt more confused than ever. I knew I could not allow these unresolved feelings to continue in our relationship, yet I couldn't disclose them to her. To do so would have been admitting to living a lie. I could hardly admit that to myself. After seriously dating for about six months, we broke up.

Over the next couple of years in college, I began to form some good friendships with some other male students. I admired their character, and we seemed to be able to share a lot of similar spiritual and personal interests. As a few of us chose to room together, I felt for the first time a kind of mutual camaraderie among male peers. The fact that I never felt sexually attracted to them made me feel safe to be in close relationship with them. Yet I could never feel safe enough to let someone else know of the wrestling going on inside.

Upon graduation, still with great confusion inside, I made another life-changing decision. Since the prospect of marriage was nowhere in sight, I determined to serve the Lord through missions. I felt the Lord's call and saw His guidance as the doors opened to go to Japan as part of a volunteer ministry, serving two-and-a-half years as a lay missionary and English teacher. The emotional and psychological energy that it took to focus on the radical cultural changes in Japan left little for other distractions. I did not recognize it at the time, but part of me was seeking escape from the sexual conflicts I had been feeling. While the conflict inside remained unresolved, I believe God effectively channeled my energies into useful works.

In Japan, some of the intensity of my feelings subsided, but I still felt alone and in need of a significant person in my life. I developed a genuine desire to marry and have a family, but I also felt deeply saddened by the fact that I did not have the capacity to create this. I felt ineligible and unequipped to have a true, honest, and passionate relationship with a woman. I continued to ask God to remove the homosexual feelings and desires. I also prayed that He would send me someone with whom I could just talk about who I was. I needed God to intervene, because I felt like I could not reach out from behind the wall myself. Someone else would have to come and encounter me in my sin and shame. Just as God did this through His Son, Jesus, for the world, so He would have to do it for me personally.

While in Japan, I tried to maintain contact with a few friends. One of them was Janine, the woman I had dated in college. Even after we broke up, a good friendship remained. During a visit back to the U.S. (when I still had 14 months to serve because I had extended my commitment for an additional year), I told her of my desire to commit myself to regular communication with her—and that I really cared for her. She responded positively.

I believe strongly in God's timing. Neither Janine nor I expected Him to work in the ways He did for both of our sakes.

It was during this visit that Janine shared with me some very painful issues in her life, which she had revealed to few people. She was receiving support and counseling for some deep wounds and hurts in her own life. Seeing her so vulnerable, my own feelings welled up as never before. How could I go on from this point in an honest and mutual relationship if I did not share now?

Had I waited until I felt ready to talk, I would still be in hiding. I too felt incredibly vulnerable and shameful, but with Janine, for the first time, I felt safe enough to open up. It was just a little, but it was enough to produce a crack in my wall. And when she did not reject me, I felt that I truly could let myself be known and yet be accepted. The meaning of confession took on a whole new light. The reality of the healing that was initiated through my disclosure will never be forgotten. ("Therefore confess your sins to each other and pray for each other so that you may be healed" [James 5:16].)

Although we continued to pray and support one another, we questioned whether the relationship could or should go beyond mutual sharing. Was that enough on which to build a full relationship between a man and a woman? What about the nature of the issues we were dealing with? Would they prevent a healthy relationship? We weren't sure.

Over the next few months, letters and cassette tapes containing pieces of the deepest places of our hearts flew back and forth across the Pacific Ocean. They were filled with soul-wrenching expressions and revelations. I suppose at first these letters were mostly a way to unburden ourselves, whether anybody read them or not. But our occasional long-distance phone calls brought to reality that each of us was actually in contact with a live person—and we found ourselves longing to have face-to-face contact.

Gradually I realized that my desires for Janine were changing. There was something about the level of intimacy at which we were sharing that was drawing us close—in a way neither of us was necessarily looking for or expecting.

A trip to Japan that Janine and her folks had been planning for quite a while came to a timely reality about six months after we had first begun to share our true selves. Seeing each other in person again illuminated that something in our relationship had changed. We had known each other for nearly eight years, but for the first time I felt that I was really known by her and she by me.

The three weeks of her visit in Japan were spent in both light conversation and deep sharing. I found a real pleasure and joy in being with her. I was comfortable with her. I could be who I really was without fear of rejection. I also felt free to love her for her true self. Through Janine, the love, acceptance, and forgiveness of Jesus were being known in a fresh way.

During my last eight months in Japan, once again by myself, I read books that I never knew existed, books that dealt with homosexuality and the Christian. I soaked up the words like a thirsty sponge and received a lot of hope. Christ began to work in a new and deeper way than I had ever experienced. And during my last visit to the U.S. before returning home permanently, I finally made contact with a Christian counselor to work through my homosexual feelings—and I felt safe. Comforted that God would continue His work in me while in Japan, I returned there to fulfill my commitment. I thank the Lord not only for the work I was privileged to do in Japan but also for the work He did in me.

Two months after moving back to the U.S., I asked Janine to marry me. I knew I loved her, and I had a genuine desire and care for her more than I thought I could have for any person. Janine prayerfully considered my request and committed herself to me. The six months of engagement were spent planning our wedding and, more important, planning our marriage. We saw our pastor and a counselor and invested time in learning skills for a good marriage. We were also able to talk openly about the issues that would specifically affect us. We were continually affirmed in our decision and felt in step with God's timing.

For me marriage has been rich and fulfilling—far more so than I had ever imagined it could be. The love and the desire I have for Janine is very deep and genuine. Yet wearing a wedding ring does not remove the issues and temptations peculiar to one who has struggled with homosexuality. The ongoing love and support that I receive in the body of Christ is very important as I continue to deal with who I am. Bringing the cross into the deepest struggle of my life has made profound changes, and even the homosexual temptations and issues lessen as time goes by. The real change, though, has been in my understanding of the Gospel. I know and experience what it really means to be loved and forgiven—and clean!

For Discussion

1. At times the author describes conflicting feelings, feelings that seem to fight each other. Describe these feelings. Have you experienced conflicting feelings as you have struggled with your own desires or the lifestyle choices of a friend or loved one? If you feel comfortable doing so, describe some of these feelings.

2. How does St. Paul's description of his life compare to the conflicting feelings the author has experienced? See Romans 7:15–24.

3. Although St. Paul acknowledges his struggle with sin and temptation in his life, he does not face these without hope. He confesses power to resist temptation, power that conquers sin. Describe this power after reading Romans 7:25.

4. By the power of the Holy Spirit working through God's Word, God enables us to echo Paul's words as we confess past sins and as we face new temptations—"Who will rescue me from this body of death? Thanks be to God—through Jesus Christ our Lord!" How does this fact affect you as you recall past sins? as you struggle with conflicting feelings? as you struggle to resist temptation?

5. Read 2 Timothy 3:16–17. How might additional opportunities to read and to study God's Word benefit you or the person who struggles with homosexuality? In what additional opportunities can you participate so that you "may be thoroughly equipped for every good work"?

2

The Roots

The lack of knowledge about the cause and origin of homosexuality has caused a lot of fear and confusion. Who knows where it comes from? Or when? Or why? Is it something I did? Was it the environment or parents? Are homosexuals born that way? Who or what is to blame? Or if there is no blame, then what? I know the questions well. So do many other people, parents of homosexuals included.

Publicly naming the cause of homosexuality has become an explosive topic in our society, particularly in politics and religion. The political tension stems from the issue of equal rights and legitimacy. Determining the cause and whether homosexuality is immutable or a matter of choice will help shape legal and public policy, especially as it regards children. In religion, determining the cause makes the difference between a blessing and a curse. The question in the homosexual's mind is, if people are born homosexual, is it really a sin? How could God expect them to behave in any other way than He made them? But if it's a choice, how should the church react?

Homosexuality: A Result of the Fall

Adam and Eve were created perfect. But in choosing to disobey Him, they both separated themselves from God and brought all of creation under a curse. Their fall subjected all people to sin, and all creation was bent toward corruption. True, we still can recognize God's intricate design and order in creation—in its beauty, in the intricacies of our bodies, in life itself. But we can see also the damage of sin and the curse on nature: natural disasters, birth defects, illness, death itself.

God's original design and plan was not only much better than we see creation today, it was perfect. But mankind did fall, and we are left with the consequences of Adam and Eve's sin as well as the *responsibility* for our own sin. Yet we simply cannot free ourselves from its dominion. As a result, the more we realize the extent of our depravity and need, the more we realize the extent of the work of grace wrought by our Savior, Jesus.

I rehearse these facts to preface our discussion on the causes of homosexuality and the question of what is "natural." Everything that now seems natural, normal, or common is, in reality, part of a fallen world.

The rest of humanity may think that what is "natural" should be the norm for life. As Christians, however, we recognize that the effects of sin are still at work within nature and humankind. Birth defects, disease, and disasters are all certainly "natural"—that is, they are not unusual. However, to call them "normal" and consider them acceptable—or even desirable—would be irrational. But that's exactly how some would have us understand homosexual feelings and desires. Without the context of recognizing God as the Creator who made a perfect world and that this world is now in a fallen state, people will continue to set the standard of what is right.

Christians can honestly look at and be open to objective truths that can be known about homosexuality. Whether we find that sin has affected us through biology or environment, we can still maintain a biblical understanding of God's original intent and design for sexual expression. Understanding sin and its effect on us as people and on nature does not excuse what has come about since the fall. However, ironically, it gives an even clearer picture of our need for God's work of salvation and restoration.

Does Biology Determine Homosexuality?

How much are one's desires, drives, and emotions determined by free choice and how much by biological condition? Apart from legal and religious argumentation, the average heterosexual does not seem to give much thought to the question. But the one who struggles with homosexuality does, for the answers are spiritually pivotal.

Within the last few years, quite a bit of attention has been given to the notion that sexual orientation is inborn. Because a few studies claimed to have found evidence of a biological link to homosexuality, the idea has become quite popular (although clearly not universally believed). If true, the finding would place sexual orientation on the same plane as race and gender in the establishment of equal rights and antidiscrimination laws. The line of reasoning says that if a condition is normal, then it can't really be wrong. And if there is nothing wrong with it, there should be no laws against it. In fact (the argument continues), laws should be made to protect against discrimination.

Truthfully, at this time, there is no conclusive evidence that homosexuality is biologically determined or caused by genetic code, no matter how the media summarizes the research. Consider the work done by Simon LeVay. Studying the brains of 41 human cadavers, 19 belonging to reported homosexual men, he claimed to have found a physical difference in part of the hypothalamus (assumed to regulate sexual activity). That part was found to be smaller in the brains of the homosexual men as compared to the brains of heterosexual men.[1]

While I cannot verify the reliability and the validity of LeVay's research, I can say that a difference in size does not prove any cause-and-effect relationship from hypothalamus to homosexuality. To conclude that is stretching the facts. Not even LeVay claims a causal relationship. Second, to apply the findings to the general population would also be erroneous. Although most of the subjects had died of AIDS-related illness, no one studied whether or not the disease or even the death itself caused (or contributed to) the size of the hypothalamus in the cadavers. So you see this study did not conclude that people are born homosexual.

A study of twins done by Michael Bailey and Richard Pillard, published in 1991, compared fraternal twin pairs with identical twin pairs. When one person in a twin pair was identified as homosexual, they found that the other's chances of being homosexual was more than twice as high among identical twins than among fraternal twins. As identical twins share the same genetic code, it is said that this demonstrates a genetic connection to the development of homosexuality.[2] Yet even in this study, hereditary factors could not be shown to account fully for the development of a homosexual orientation in males. The researchers themselves say that as much as 26–69 percent of male homosexual orientation could be attributed to something other than heredity. Even more problematic is Bailey's own statement that there is no guarantee that the sample for this study would be the same as one systematically selected from a well-specified population. In other words, if the study focused on a sample of volunteers that in some way was not representative of all twins, it is impossible to account accurately for any differences.

(While these two studies have gained a great deal of public attention, a plethora of research on homosexuality goes relatively unnoticed. If this is an area of interest to you, I encourage you to look into the other resources offered at the end of this book.)

If then there is no solid evidence for direct biological or hereditary cause for homosexuality, could there be biological factors that may *predispose* a person toward homosexual desires? Considering this possibility is threatening, particularly for Christians. It seems more biblical to believe that people who have homosexual desires always choose to be that way. After all, if homosexual feelings and attractions are beyond one's control, would that not remove responsibility for actions? And wouldn't that excuse homosexual relationships?

The moral issue for Christians, however, is not whether homosexual feelings and desires are either by nature or by nurture, but whether or not a person chooses to engage in homosexual activity. Those who look for justification in biology are offering the excuse "I can't help myself." But that claim contradicts another excuse, that this is all between "consenting adults." The latter is true, at least insofar as those who engage in homosexual behavior (apart from being forced to) do so with their own consent. We are responsible for the ways we choose to act out sexually.

Perhaps the real truth about the homosexual condition is similar to what we know about alcoholism. A good deal of evidence points to hereditary factors. This, however, does not mean that all people who suffer from alcoholism have such a predisposition. Also, it does not mean that a person who has a predisposition will, in fact, become an alcoholic. Finally, as common as alcoholism is, we still do not consider it "normal."

Consider again the question whether heredity should be a reason to legitimize homosexuality. It doesn't for alcoholism, even though a much greater body of evidence shows that alcoholism has some hereditary or genetic factors. Why then is alcoholism considered a disease and treated as such, but homosexuality is supposed to be condoned as an acceptable, alternative lifestyle? The standards are very different.

Take the next logical step and you can see how illogical it is to excuse behavior on the basis of heredity. The realm of human sexual experience is not limited to heterosexuality or homosexuality but includes sexual desires for children (pedophilia), animals (zoophilia or bestiality), and even the dead (necrophilia). Some on the fringes of society claim that these too are genetically predetermined. Common sense and our own experiences bear out what Scripture says by implication: that our sexuality is not so predetermined by genetics or biology that we cannot but help to behave in that way. When it comes to sexual behavior, all people—even heterosexuals—make decisions. Granted, decisions made in accordance with what God has designed and intended for our sexuality may be much more difficult for some people than for others. But the decision is still ours whether or not to live by God's plan for sexual activity: only within a monogamous, heterosexual marriage. That decision every adult has to make, homosexual or not.

Does Environment Create Homosexuality?

Before we discuss the role of environment/nurture and a person's sexual desires, keep in mind that no one consciously decides to be sexually attracted to a certain gender. Nobody wakes up one morning in early adolescence and says, "I think I want to be homosexual/heterosexual/necrophiliac/whatever." It's as absurd as it sounds. Homosexual desires come about as "naturally" as do heterosexual ones. A person's choice has little, if anything, to do with it. I know that if it were a simple matter of choice, I would not have chosen to have the desires for the same sex. Like any sexual desires, they were just a part of me. I'm not arguing in favor of heredity as a cause of the feelings; the fact is, I don't know where my feelings came from.

In spite of the unwilling appearance of homosexual feelings, some sort of developmental process seems to foster its emergence. Although sexual or erotic desires usually do not emerge until early adolescence, a great deal of early learning and activity shapes our gender identity and its formation—so much, in fact, that no one can detail every specific factor integral to our development. Homosexual theories based on environmental factors have included ideas about parents, sexual abuse, pornography, poor experiences with the opposite sex, masturbation, and sexual behavior, besides others. A great deal of information can be found on the myriad of environmental factors. And because so many experiences play some role in homosexual formation, blame cannot be laid to any given childhood situation (or parents in particular). While some patterns in familial relationships and some childhood experiences can be identified among many who struggle with homosexuality, similar patterns can be identified in backgrounds of people who do not.

The difficulty of trying to determine real causes of homosexuality arises from the fact that each person is a unique individual. Life does not follow a recipe with simple step-by-step instructions. Besides all of the different events that shape a person (and they vary from person to person, identical twins as well), each individual gives unique responses to those unique situations and circumstances.

Joe Dallas' book *Desires in Conflict* suggests that the popular theories regarding the development of homosexuality tend to be misleading. They wrongly assume that the same reasons underlie all people who struggle with homosexuality. In actuality, the roots vary from person to person. What may have been a critical factor for one person may not have been for another. Children in they same family may respond differently to any given circumstance. Dallas writes:

> I will offer a few common patterns I've seen in the development of homosexuality. Instead of one universal cause, I've seen a consistent developmental pattern. Specifically, I've come to believe that homosexual attractions develop within a simple process:

1. A child's perception of his or her relationship to parents or significant others.
2. A child's emotional response to those perceptions.
3. Emotional needs arising from these perceptions and responses.
4. The sexualization of those emotional needs.[3]

Dallas does not emphasize the events or circumstances that did or did not occur in a child's life. Instead he focuses on the perceptions and the responses. Two factors help explain the diversity of histories among men and women who struggle with homosexuality: (1) Children perceive a given circumstance in numerous ways; and (2) their unique response is not the only one possible. This is not to say that parent-child interaction is unimportant. The contrary is true, even though a great deal of study and research in this area gets pushed aside as people focus on the more recent and popular biological and hereditary theories.

Joseph Nicolosi, a therapist specializing in the area of male homosexuality, blends together many long-standing theories that speak to the issue of parent and child dynamics. Nicolosi emphasized particularly the importance of the father and son relationship and how early gender identity is formed in males. Where a significant deficit in relationship exists, a boy experiencing the void may later experience an eroticized version of the need.[4] Before Nicolosi, Elizabeth Moberly recognized the same underlying principle:

> [T]he homosexual—whether man or woman—has suffered from some deficit in the relationship with the parent of the same sex; and that there is a corresponding drive to make good this deficit—through the medium of same-sex or "homosexual" relationships.[5]

Moberly also proposed that when a relationship is breached, the child develops a "defensive detachment." While this stance initially serves to avoid the hurt of broken relationship, it later hinders the restoration of relationship in healthy and legitimate ways.

Although both Nicolosi and Moberly talk about the importance of the parent-child relationship, neither of them blames the actions of the parent as a cause. The reasons why children may emotionally detach from mother or father are many and varied. In some cases, they might be known and understandable, but in others the reasons may never be known. Known or not, we need to remember that the child's response is more crucial than the circumstances.

The Shortcomings of Research

No shortage exists of statistics used to support almost any view regarding the development of sexuality. As a society, we have become enamored with numbers, believing that if something is supported with real figures, it must be true. We often forget, however, to evaluate how those numbers were obtained. Too often we assume that all research uses proper and fair methods and that there is no bias. If something is in print, then it must be valid. We need to be open but also discerning.

Doing research in the area of homosexuality presents a number of basic problems. First, no objective instrument exists to determine one's sexual orientation. Therefore, researchers tend to define sexual orientation based on behavior. However, behavior is not always an accurate indicator of what is occurring inside. Therefore, researchers have to depend on people to report on themselves truthfully—a difficult assignment, given the attitudes of our society.

Second, most of what is known about homosexuality has been shared by a select group of people: those willing to talk about their sexuality. It would be hard to count the other men and women who struggle secretly with their sexual identity. Without knowing who they are, it's impossible to measure their feelings and behaviors. Many will not even take the risk of giving information anonymously.

Third, no one would (or should) condone the kind of scientific experimentation done on things: subjecting them to various influences to see what the outcome might be. Yet this kind of testing produces the most reliable information about cause and effect.

To summarize: Although studies are being done in the area of homosexual formation, we need to remember that the statistics, and the research itself, are based primarily on only one subclass of homosexuals and what they say about themselves. True, some studies have observed family dynamics over a long period of time, but even these studies cannot report beyond what the people say about themselves. No one can measure every event in a family's life, and no one can measure how a child interprets and responds in his or her heart to every event. Therefore, much research in the area of homosexuality is merely theory, based on partial information provided by people who do not represent the entire class to which they belong.

One more point, beyond whether or not the statistics are accurate: The cause-and-effect roots of homosexual orientation are not as simple to deal with as that of, for example, smallpox. We have come to expect that once "science" knows the cause of something we want to avoid, we can simply vaccinate against that cause. I too used to feel that if I just knew where the feelings came from, then I could fix myself and move on. It has not been so simple. Yes, it has been insightful to learn about how homosexual feelings develop and to look at the ways I responded to certain situations and feelings. Whether or not these fall into a cause-and-effect category I cannot say; but this is not where the healing has come from anyway. Rather, God alone graciously brings healing and hope to people. He is the one who brings change.

For Discussion

1. People today, possibly more than ever before, try to find someone or something to blame for difficulties that may occur in their lives. What evidence can you give to show that many people today play the "blame game"?

2. The apostle Paul records that God's grace is made perfect in weakness. As God enters our weakness, He changes us, strengthening us with the power His grace provides. What danger do people face if they blame their sinful thoughts, words, or actions on someone or something? See 1 John 1:8. How could failure to take responsibility for sin ultimately endanger a person's salvation?

3. What does God offer to all who confess their sins? See 1 John 1:9.

4. What assurance does 1 John 1:9 provide that blame or denial of sin can never provide? Suppose new studies indicate a strong genetic factor linked to homosexuality. React to this discovery as you reflect on sin and God's grace.

5. How is confession of sin a beginning for healing and recovery for a person burdened by sin? What hope for the future does the person who has experienced the magnitude of God's grace and mercy through faith in Jesus have as he or she considers the future here on earth? in eternity?

3

God's Intent for Our Sexuality

The home in which my wife and I live has the old style double-hung wood windows with ropes attached to counterweights inside the window frame. Since some of the ropes have long since broken, the windows cannot remain open. One day we propped open one window with a wooden spoon, and this solved our problem evermore. Because of this simple remedy, the broken rope does not bother us, and we have no reason to go to the trouble of repairing it. As a matter of fact, we really do not think any more about the fact that it is broken. And to replace the whole window is neither worth the trouble nor the expense. Our solution is an easy and convenient one, but obviously the spoon is not being used for the purpose for which it was made, nor do the windows function in the way that they were intended and designed to.

I don't know whether or not the makers of the window and the spoon really care about how my wife and I have decided to use the things they have made. But I do know that God, who created my wife and me, certainly cares about how we use ourselves and our bodies. It is for this reason that we need to consider God's intent for us as man and woman. Without dealing with the whole picture of our intended and proper sexuality, it would be worthless to try to address why God so clearly addresses the issue of homosexuality in Scripture. That "whole picture" includes, of course, Genesis 1:28: "Be fruitful and increase in number." But that's only part of our identity as men and women.

The Image of God

> Then God said, "Let Us make man in Our image, in Our likeness." ... So God created man in His own image, in the image of God He created him; male and female He created them. (Genesis 1:26–27)

Scripture does not say that the purpose of human existence is the expression of its sexuality. Still, as the above passage intimates, our sexuality clearly is part of our identity in relation to the one who created us. Within our identities as male and female and through the unity of the two, the very image of God is in some way reflected or known. Plus, by looking at the creation account, we can see part of God's intent for us as sexual beings.

> The Lord God said, "It is not good for the man to be alone. I will make a helper suitable for him." ... So the Lord God caused the man to fall into a deep sleep; and while he was sleeping, He took one of the man's ribs and closed up the place with flesh. Then the Lord God made a woman from the rib He had taken out of the man, and He brought her to the man. The man said, "This is now bone of my bones and flesh of my flesh; she shall be called 'woman,' for she was taken out of man." For this reason a man will leave his father and mother and be united to his wife, and they will become one flesh. (Genesis 2:18, 21–24)

Clearly, God the designer destined people for relatedness. While we can say very little about Adam before the creation of Eve, we can be sure he had a perfect relationship with God and the rest of creation. In God's eyes, though, that was not enough. "It is not good for the man to be alone."

Note what God does next. In His wisdom, He did not see fit to simply create the perfect companion for Adam with "Let there be," as He created the animals. Nor did He scoop up the dust of the earth and breathe life into this new being. Instead,

God chose to perform a unique and beautiful creative act as He took out a rib from Adam in order to create Eve. God "divided" the whole Adam and brought forth man and woman, masculine and feminine, plurality in union. God divided one into two, so that they might draw together again as one. He intended for us to be attracted and drawn into relation with a complementary "other."

How poignantly this illustrates God's image as a triune God! In the union of two lives, male and female, we see singularity in the midst of plurality. And just as God's plurality brought forth humanity, so humanity's plurality brings forth its offspring. The family unit, in some way, though not fully, mirrors the image of God.

As I continue to ponder the idea that man and woman share the same flesh and that God blesses the coming together of male and female, I understand more clearly how homosexuality does not fit into the picture of proper and holy sexuality. At their heart and foundation, homosexual relationships distort the image of God. Such a relationship cannot possibly mirror the revelation of Himself as a single, complementary union. Individuals engaging in homosexual union cannot encounter each other as "other" but only as undifferentiated and merely as the same. This comes very close to the kind of self-love God condemns, because it tries to minimize the distinction between the subject and the object of love. We are to love one another, not because we are the same but in spite of our differences. Only then can we begin to understand the immeasurable love God has for us humans.

Significant too is that life proceeds as a product and blessing from heterosexual union but cannot possibly come from homosexual union. We cannot transcend the distinction God made between male and female in order that, among other purposes, we humans might participate with Him in the creation of children. Not that all marriages have to or can result in children; God has not made that possible. However, His design is clear: "So God created man in His own image, in the image of God He created him; male and female He created them. God blessed them and said to them, 'Be fruitful and increase in number' " (Genesis 1:27–28).

Homosexuality and the Law of God

In light of why God created sexuality, we can see why He condemns homosexuality. Because our sexuality is such a precious gift to be shared in relationship, God has provided specific guidelines and laws for the sake of our good. Outside of what God has designed is not only sinful but is bound to go awry. God's Law is not given in a vacuum; though if it were, it still would have to be obeyed. Rather, God provided His Law in order that His purposes might be accomplished—in the case of sexuality, unity in diversity.

We, however, turn away from the Lord and His blessings—a process described in Romans 1:21–32. Within our fallen state as descendants of Adam and Eve, humankind progresses farther away from all that which is of God. First, God is not recognized for all that He is and has done; then hearts are darkened and thinking becomes futile. Idolatry sets in and other gods are created. Finally, God allows for people to be given over to their own desires and passions.

> God gave them over to shameful lusts. Even their women exchanged natural relations for unnatural ones. In the same way the men also abandoned natural relations with women and were inflamed with lust for one another. Men committed indecent acts with other men, and received in themselves the due penalty for their perversion. (Romans 1:26–27)

One popular argument today says that when homosexual relations feel natural, a person should not try to pursue heterosexual relations, for that would be unnatural. How far from the truth! Not only does God tell us through Paul what is natural and what is not, our own common sense knows that the natural purpose of sexuality, procreation, can be accomplished only through what is natural from creation: the natural complementary function of the male and female genitalia.

One reinterpretation of the Old Testament points with approval to what some contrive as a homosexual relationship between David and Jonathan. However, there is no indication of any sexual relationship at all. Rather, Scripture portrays them as expressing a deep and honorable love that they shared, one that should not be construed as something other than a holy, compassionate, and exemplary friendship.

Another ploy tries to explain away what happened at and to Sodom and Gomorrah (Genesis 19:1–26) as different from the traditional understanding—especially since the word *homosexual* is not used in the account. The claim is made that Sodom was destroyed because of its inhospitality toward Lot rather than its great evil, which included homosexual behavior. A straightforward reading of the passage leaves no doubt as to its intention. And this happened *before* the Law was given to Moses and the Israelites.

That written Law also specifically addressed and condemned homosexual relationships by name in Leviticus 18:22 and 20:13. In these passages God clearly calls male homosexuality detestable and worthy of death. The struggle to escape this biblical ban against homosexual behavior frequently points to such New Testament passages as Mark 7:19 and Acts 10:14–15, which suggest that Christians are no longer subject to Old Testament laws. The argument ignores that Scripture differentiates between the dietary and ceremonial laws (which have been set aside) and the moral law, which is upheld and reiterated in the New Testament (Mark 7:20–23; Matthew 5:27–28).

The biblical prohibition against homosexual behavior is not an outdated, Old Testament ban. The Romans 1 section clearly belies this. So does, for example, 1 Corinthians 6:9–10, which lists those who will not inherit the kingdom of God:

> Do you not know that the wicked will not inherit the kingdom of God? Do not be deceived: Neither the sexually immoral nor idolaters nor adulterers nor male prostitutes nor homosexual offenders nor thieves nor the greedy nor drunkards nor slanderers nor swindlers will inherit the kingdom of God.

Some have argued that the translation of the word for "homosexual" (*arsenokoitēs*) is not accurate and that Paul was not actually condemning homosexuality but rather a perversion of it in the form of male prostitution. However, as Dallas has pointed out,

> *Arsenokoitēs* is derived from two Greek words—*arsēn*, meaning "male," and *koitē*, meaning "couch" or "bed," usually with a sexual connotation, as in Hebrews 13:4: "Marriage is honorable in all, and the bed *(koitē)* undefiled" (KJV). The combination of the two terms does not suggest prostitution—only sexual contact between two men.[1]

As one can see, the Bible soundly condemns homosexual behavior; not only specifically but also as part of a general prohibition against any sexual behavior between people apart from a monogamous, heterosexual marriage.

Significantly, sexual relations between two people of the same gender is never blessed or condoned in Scripture.

Getting the Whole Picture

Scripture as a whole is clear about what God intends for us as beings created in His image. The Lord does not regard the sin of homosexuality as the worst sin and make it a huge focus of attention. Nor does He dismiss it or think lightly of it. Instead He gives us a very balanced understanding of our sexuality and who we are as engendered beings. God celebrates, blesses, and takes delight in our persons as male and female and has made a very special way that His image is expressed through the union of a man and a woman.

Using the analogy of the malfunctioning window in our home and our use of the wooden spoon to keep it open, a homosexual relationship can seem to function "good enough." After a while, a person may even believe that there is not really anything wrong or strange. I have heard many say that homosexual relationships "feel natural"—and therefore, that they are natural. This grieves me. I know that homosexual activity is not only sinful, but that God has created our sexuality for our good, for our pleasure, and for producing life. This is not fully realized in homosexual behavior.

C. S. Lewis writes about how we often settle for less than what God has provided for us.

> If we consider the unblushing promises of reward and the staggering nature of the rewards promised in the Gospels, it would seem that our Lord finds our desires, not too strong, but too weak. We are half-hearted creatures, fooling about with drink and sex and ambition when infinite joy is offered us, like an ignorant child who wants to go on making mud pies in a slum because he cannot imagine what is meant by the offer of a holiday at the sea. We are far too easily pleased.[2]

I understand very much how homosexual desires and feelings can feel natural and how it seems that homosexual behavior would fulfill the very strongly felt longings and needs. But God has called us into a holy love relationship with Himself and with others. Jesus summed all of the laws and the prophets into two commandments: "Love the Lord your God with all your heart and with all your soul and with all your mind and with all your strength" and "Love your neighbor as yourself" (Mark 12:30–31). A sexual relationship is not an expression of love to share with whomever we see fit. It is a physical expression that flows from a deeply committed and intimate relationship that should begin with God.

For Discussion

1. In His Word God condemns sin. We call this condemnation of sin God's Law. Why do people who have caved into their sinful desires often seek disclaimers or loopholes in God's Word? Are there any disclaimers or loopholes that the author provides? Why?

2. Why is any attempt to justify sin dangerous to the spiritual well-being of a person?

3. What is the ultimate fate for those who fail to keep God's Law? See Romans 6:23. What danger does the person who is secure in his or her sin ultimately face?

4. What does God provide to those who repent of their sin? Review 1 John 1:9.

5. God provides complete forgiveness through faith in Jesus to repentant sinners. What must a repentant sinner do in order to receive God's forgiveness? See Ephesians 2:8–9.

6. How might God use you, or has God used you, to share His Law and His Gospel (the Good News of forgiveness through faith in Jesus)? How can God use the opportunities you have to share Law and Gospel to transform lives tainted or wallowing in sin?

4

The Process of Healing

> Do not be deceived: Neither the sexually immoral nor idolaters nor adulterers nor male prostitutes nor homosexual offenders nor thieves nor the greedy nor drunkards nor slanderers nor swindlers will inherit the kingdom of God. And that is what some of you were. But you were washed, you were sanctified, you were justified in the name of the Lord Jesus Christ and by the Spirit of our God. (1 Corinthians 6:9–11)

People who struggle with homosexuality have probably read, heard, or seen in the media that nothing can be done to change. This needs to be challenged. People can change—and do! Right now, hundreds of people with homosexual feelings are pursuing God's intent for their sexuality. Across America and around the world, specialized church ministries, counselors, professional therapists, and para-church organizations are successfully helping people who desire to deal with their homosexuality. There has also been a dramatic growth in the amount of information available in the form of books, newsletters, audiocassette tapes, and videos. As a matter of fact, the growth of ministries and the availability of materials has made the concept of leaving homosexuality appear as a new phenomenon.

The truth is, people have been turning away from homosexuality at least since the beginning of the Christian church and probably long before. Clearly, some people in fellowship in the early Corinthian church had practiced homosexual behavior. These Paul graciously reminds that, yes, in spite of the fact that they had practiced sinful ways, "You were washed, you were sanctified, you were justified in the name of the Lord Jesus Christ and by the Spirit of our God." That is still true. God's mercy, grace, forgiveness, and healing are present today as they have been through all history.

Exodus International is an example of how God is working through the church to address the special needs of such people.[1] Its leaders and members have reached out to support and assist the change of those who have homosexual feelings and who have been involved in homosexual behavior.

At the same time, we need to recognize that the definition of "change" varies from person to person. Some but not all homosexuals have never experienced any other feelings. Some but not all have never acted out their orientation. Some feel very strong attractions; others, weak ones. Looking from the outside, no one is able to evaluate whether an individual homosexual person has changed enough to be called "healed." Only the individual can say, "I have changed." Even then, the person usually cannot claim a complete change. Rather, the measure needs to be that the frequency of desires have lessened over time and that their intensity is not as powerful.

On the other hand, some people inside and outside the church believe that those who experience sexual attractions toward people of the same sex cannot change their desires. It is suggested that instead of even trying to change, one should learn to accept homosexual desires and seek to find fulfilling sexual relationship(s) with those of the same sex. Saving that topic for later, this chapter discusses two key questions about change and healing: "What really does it mean for someone to be healed of homosexuality?" and "How does change take place?"

What Does It Mean to Change?

People generally seem to believe that changing sexual *orientation* means simply changing feelings and behavior. Even I thought that at one time. If I could just get this piece of my sexuality to fit into the puzzle of my life, I would be fine.

This sounds very logical and appropriate, but it is also very simplistic. True, changing orientation does involve changing behavior. Some would even suggest that feelings do not really matter anyway. Just stop acting out on the desires, and everything will be all right. Many have tried to do just this. They repent of their sin, stop their behavior, and then believe that their homosexuality is all "healed."

This "quick fix" attitude and the expectation that homosexual issues can be resolved through a sinner's prayer or an emotional experience of recommitment often leaves the struggling person alone and isolated. The behavior ceases and is under control for a season; but when a fall back into sin occurs, the person feels, "I thought that the Lord healed me of this." And the shame or guilt often keeps the person from remaining in Christian fellowship. He or she feels unworthy of the continued acceptance really needed, and the healing process is often abandoned long before evidence of a real change begins to appear.

Healing and change always require more than ceasing certain behaviors. The scribes and Pharisees probably behaved very well from all outside appearances, but Jesus also called them "whitewashed tombs" and "full of dead men's bones" (Matthew 23:27). Jesus was not saying that behavior does not matter, but to focus solely on outside appearances without considering the evils and wickedness of the heart is true hypocrisy.

Behavior is important, but more needs to be considered. Restraint from acting out homosexual orientation is partially a cause and partially an effect of the healing process. In other words, a change in behavior will help in the process of inner healing; but probably more so, behavior change results from heart change. God desires for us to bear good fruit of sexual purity and wholeness, to demonstrate outwardly inner sexual integrity.

One aspect of change that I did not really expect or look for was that my focus and perception in life drastically changed. The way I understand myself as a man has changed. My understanding of my relationship with the Lord has changed. The way that I know, understand, and accept His grace has changed. I thought my problem was just a little puzzle piece that would not fit in the right way. I came to realize that actually a great deal of the puzzle was not put together the way it should have been.

My homosexual thoughts and my feelings of self-hatred had been ever present in my life. When I began to work through the issues of my homosexual attractions in a deep and honest way with the Lord and in relation with others, I became less obsessed with the problems. I began to realize that I was not the only one in the world who had the same problem. I no longer needed to expend the emotional energy trying to hide, maintain a good front, and repress all the desires that bound me with shame. My whole perspective and perception of my sexuality, manhood, and relation with God has been the best and biggest aspect of my change.

Most important, I came to recognize that healing is not a goal to be attained but rather a process to be entered into. And once entered by addressing the core issues in heart and life, change and growth are going to happen. That change may not be what we thought we wanted, but with God's grace it will be what we need. I encourage every homosexual to pursue wholeheartedly the process of change that God offers.

How Does Change Take Place?

A ministry group to which I have been tied has humorously mentioned a be-made-normal wand. We have fun thinking about how wonderful it would be just to wave a magic wand over someone wanting to change, and—poof—instantaneous and effortless heterosexuality! What an easy solution to a complex and difficult process that takes time!

Commitment, effort, and dedication to a process over time—this is the general rule of the way God brings change and healing, development and growth, step-by-step. Yes, God can bring about sudden and miraculous change, and I even know someone who can personally testify to this. However, this is not the rule. Instead, there seem to be significant stages through which people will go. There are also some specific issues that seem to be particular to the diminishing of the desires and attractions and then leaving homosexuality. These steps include (1) facing crisis; (2) identifying the motive; (3) opening up; (4) defining the new self; and (5) forming new friendships.

Facing Crisis

Denial keeps most homosexuals well defended against recognizing the seriousness of problems in our lives. Then some crisis happens, and we start to see the reality and/or magnitude of reality. The crisis may not be traumatic; it could be a small thing. It could be "the straw that broke the camel's back," if precipitating factors have accumulated for a long time. In whatever event, the person is actually forced for some reason(s) to face the truth.

For me, that crisis was when my later-to-be-wife, Janine, shared with me some very deep wounds and hurts through which she was working. When she talked of the deep matters of sin and shame in her life, I felt convicted of the things in my life that I had never shared. That was a crisis for me, because I had to make a decision to share and name my problem *in the presence of another person.* Had I not said anything, I'm not sure I would have ever come out of my denial.

The crises of some people are far more difficult and intense than mine. I have seen people recognizing their need when their marriage or same-sex relationship began to fall apart. Some have been "caught in the act" or found out through unexpected ways. Finally, for some, the crisis came simply—when a book, magazine article, or TV program opened their eyes to the availability of help for their deepening anxieties and struggles.

Identifying the Motive

In every person's case there are almost always one or two clearly identifiable factors that help to bring them out of denial and onto a journey toward growth and healing. The crisis, in turn, seems to determine the motivation that one has to persevere with the ongoing process. Some are motivated because of pressure from others: family members; church; society; or other friends who will only accept them if they are "normal." Others are motivated out of fear: of AIDS or other diseases; of "being caught"; or even of eternal damnation.

While these are common sources, one particular motivation seems to result in the deepest and most effectual healing: the knowledge that there must be a better way. Those who are thus motivated want to pursue health for an unhindered relationship with God and for their own peace of mind. When by His grace God draws someone to repent, it is accompanied by the realization of God's presence in the midst of the struggle.

Experiencing and practicing the working presence of Jesus Christ in the midst of the struggle was a new thing for me. I had grown up knowing that Jesus died on the cross to forgive my sins and grant me free salvation, but I did not know how to live out this grace in the most secret area of my heart. I had instead been practicing a more legalistic approach in response to guilty feelings. I felt that God would leave me and not accept me in times of sin and guilt. He was a watchful judge.

Therefore, I would try to stop my homosexual thoughts and fantasies and my other behaviors so that God would really accept me and I could approach Him.

Then, in the middle of temptation and in the middle of my shame, I experienced Jesus' love through others—and my motivation changed. I was no longer fearful of the Lord's rejection of me as a person. The experience happened as I began to share with others my heart. I would share my failings and my shame, and I would receive the declaration of God's grace and experience the ongoing love, respect, and acceptance of me as a person and as a real man.

By hearing the real voices and feeling the real touch and embraces of brothers and sisters in Christ, I experienced the reality of Christ's presence in my life.

Opening Up

A third factor necessary for change is to reveal to someone both one's sexual orientation and the desire to change. The process of change is so difficult and risk-laden that the homosexual needs the understanding and support of at least one other person. Some choose to disclose themselves to a pastor, relative, close friend, or counselor. Others find that too threatening, so they contact a specialized ministry as a safe place to take the first step of talking openly about the problem. More important than the category of person is simply finding someone with whom to risk vulnerability in order to draw on that person's support and strength amid the guilt and shame.

This step, though, frightens every homosexual who wants to change. Fear and isolation, believing the problem too shameful, unforgivable, or too big for someone else to bear—these feelings only exacerbate the problem. Some are so frightened that they won't take the chance, even though they say they believe someone "out there" might be able to help. Others are so ashamed that they believe they can change themselves, on their own—which can't be done. But it's a lie that the problem is too shameful to share and that no one can be trusted. Because of what God has done for all humans in Christ Jesus, Christians who have experienced the abundance of God's grace are capable of extending His love and support for all who seek to live by His grace.

Defining the New Self

The shame that ties homosexuals to the past is tightly tied to the labels that have so long been part of the struggle. Labels such as "homosexual," "fag," "lesbian," "queer," or "dike" are deeply felt and have become part of one's identity. While heterosexuals may define themselves by their jobs or family roles, homosexuals commonly define themselves in terms of their sexuality. These deeply rooted labels need to be countered with what is true: that the Lord has called us by another name. Leanne Payne, a writer and researcher in the area of Christianity and sexual wholeness, writes:

> There is really no such thing as a "homosexual" person. There are only those who need healing of old rejections and deprivations, deliverance from the wrong kind of self-love and the actions that issue from it, and—along with that—the knowledge of their own higher selves in Christ.[2]

Like all Christians who deal with sin, though, homosexuals who are changing live with the struggle to enact what God has done. It is a continual process. As St. Paul wrote:

> So I find this law at work: When I want to do good, evil is right there with me. For in my inner being I delight in God's law; but I see another law at work in the members of my body, waging war against the law of my mind and making me a prisoner of the law of sin at work within my members. What a wretched man I am! Who will rescue me from this body of death? Thanks be to God—

through Jesus Christ our Lord! So then, I myself in my mind am a slave to God's law, but in the sinful nature a slave to the law of sin. (Romans 7:21–25)

Martin Luther, in his explanation of Baptism, describes the process:

> [T]he Old Adam in us should by daily contrition and repentance be drowned and die with all sins and evil desires, and ... a new man should daily emerge and arise to live before God in righteousness and purity forever.[3]

The new identity arises through an ongoing practice of rejecting and putting to death the old lies. This does not mean pretending the hurts, the feelings, and the painful memories do not exist. Rather, the person recognizes them and then takes action to grasp onto and hold what is true in the identity of the new man. And even though the feelings and temptations may be still real and present, the truth is that what we feel does not determine our identity. We are God's child, forgiven and transformed.

> Shall we go on sinning so that grace may increase? By no means! We died to sin; how can we live in it any longer? Or don't you know that all of us who were baptized into Christ Jesus were baptized into His death? We were therefore buried with Him through baptism into death in order that, just as Christ was raised from the dead through the glory of the Father, we too may live a new life. (Romans 6:1–4)

Forming New Friendships

Because of the shame and secrecy involved, many practicing homosexuals limit their close associations and friendships to other homosexuals, knowing they will be accepted as they are as well as reinforced in their choices. The process of change, however, requires that those who are changing develop new friendships—including and especially with members of the opposite sex.

The process is difficult. Labels such as "homosexual struggler" or "ex-gay" get in the way. So do the phantom voices that whisper, "You're not a real man/woman; if they really knew you, they wouldn't like you." Also, we're not always very trusting of people who have not gone through the struggle. Yet the affirmation we need the most often needs to come from the same people who seem most threatening to us.

It needs to be said again: The path to change includes risk. But be assured: the labels and fears will begin to lose their grip as new friendships prove them false.

I have discussed some of what I have seen occur in others' lives as well as in myself when someone begins to pursue God's intent for their identity and sexuality. I have also talked about some of the significant steps that are a part of healing and growth out of homosexuality. While this book is a good start to learn about this topic, I encourage you also to seek other sources that are dedicated to giving a far more in-depth coverage of these ideas. There are specific listings in the resource section at the end of the book.

For you who are reading this because you want to know more about your own struggle with homosexuality, I want to bless and encourage you. An easy answer or step-by-step recipe for leaving behind the feelings, behaviors, and temptations does not exist. Yet I strongly believe in the reality of healing and change in process. I pray you will begin to recognize that God's presence can be experienced in a real and intimate way as He is allowed into deep and vulnerable areas.

For Discussion

1. Describe your attitude toward change. How is your attitude toward change similar to or different from the author's?

2. Why is each step toward healing so important in the process of change? How might disregard for a step hamper the healing process?

3. What steps in the process do you consider most important? Why?

4. Reread Romans 6:1–4. Reflect on verses 1–3. How can understanding these verses help us to understand the "new life" in Christ?

5. Review Luther's words. What can you do to tap into the power of God provided to you at your Baptism? How can God through the power of the Holy Spirit transform your life?

5

The Challenge in Society

In a pluralistic and secular society, the ideas and viewpoints of this book do not hold the authority they have within the church. As a country, we have become increasingly intolerant and suspicious of biblically founded principles. We decide our morals by popular vote. This is especially evident as old laws are challenged and new ones are created. Thus, few states still have prohibitions against homosexual relationships, and nowhere are they strictly enforced.

Do Moral Norms Exist?

Society does need norms for regulating morality. In spite of the cliche´ that "you can't legislate morality," the laws of society (including those in North America) do regard as normative the immorality of (for example) stealing and killing.

As Christians, we are encouraged to work for the good of the country, even when the country rejects God and His Word. Sometimes, of course, God's Word is silent on a particular issue (for example, which political party a Christian may join). At other times God has spoken, but we need to convince the population of the wisdom of what He has said.

The task is not impossible, for humanity carries God's Law within its heart.

> When Gentiles, who do not have the law, do by nature things required by the law, they are a law for themselves, even though they do not have the law, since they show that the requirements of the law are written on their hearts, their consciences also bearing witness, and their thoughts now accusing, now even defending them. (Romans 2:14–15)

Those who violate natural law experience a great deal of inner conflict and guilt. They also suffer greatly from the contempt and scorn of others. Such inner and external pressures take their toll. So, for example,

> Homosexual men are six times more likely to have attempted suicide than heterosexual men. Between 25 and 33 percent of homosexual men and women are alcoholics (the national average is 7 percent).[1]

Note that I am not suggesting that homosexuality causes suicide and alcoholism. Rather, these problems witness to the pressure for all to obey the natural law. When that law is rejected, first- and second-level tragedies are the result.

Most people, of course, do not want to take responsibility when they violate either codified or natural law. The excuses are many: "I was temporarily insane"; "I was raised in poverty"; "It was the only way out"; "Everybody else was doing it." Those who give such rationales hope that avoiding responsibility will also eliminate society's accusations as well as inner guilt. "If I have no responsibility, then neither you nor I can make me feel guilty—and I don't have to change."

Since homosexuality is not a onetime event but an ongoing lifestyle, these rationalizations seek not to excuse behavior but to legitimize it. Powerful political activism within the homosexual community continues to push for the inclusion of "sexual preference" or "sexual orientation" on various states' laws about antidiscrimination and minority rights. These laws have traditionally protected against discrimination based on inherited human characteristics such as gender, race, or physical handicap. Laws have also sought to protect the constitutional right of freedoms of religion and speech. The homosexual community, therefore, is trying to use the same approach for legalizing its immorality.

1. *It's an inherited human characteristic.* Since homosexuals are born with a sexual orientation of being attracted to the same sex, then there should be laws against discrimination. After all, they cannot help it, and people cannot change.
2. *Freedom of religion protects me from you.* Other peoples' religious morals should not be pushed on everyone else. If my religion says that homosexuality is acceptable, who can say anything against it? Besides, it all depends on how you personally feel the Bible should be interpreted.
3. *Freedom of expression gives me the right.* There is no reason why two people who love each other and who are physically attracted toward one another should be denied the right to express their desires through physical and sexual acts.
4. *Without victims, there is no crime.* As long as people mutually consent to a sexual relationship, they are not really hurting anyone.
5. *Homophobia and bigotry against homosexuals have no place in our country.*

We can, of course, argue against each of these propositions. Behavior is under the control of the individual, in spite of whatever predisposition might be inherited. Not just religion but natural law condemns the practice of homosexuality. Freedom of expression does not give permission to say or do anything a person wants. Both natural and codified law condemn certain victimless crimes. And counterattacking with loaded words such as *homophobic* and *bigot* deliberately bypass a discussion of morality in order to pressure a person into at least silence if not social tolerance.

Argumentative attacks, however, seldom accomplish anything other than raising the other person's defenses. Homosexuals do not want to hear that their lifestyle is wrong and can be dangerous. Heterosexuals do not want to hear that they should love the sinner even while not the sin. And some people will never acknowledge the truth of God and His intent for our lives under His grace.

Where are we to stand as Christians? Do we stand up and attempt to stem the tide by actively fighting against the changing tide? Do we sit back passively and let people go ahead and do their own thing? The questions are tough, but we cannot ignore them.

The Christian Response in the Public Arena

In God's Word, God clearly tells us how He desires us to live. God would have those who love and trust in Him—as well as all others—to live in obedience to His Law. He desires those who belong to Him to take a firm stand against sin and evil evidenced in their own lives and in the lives of those around them. Further, He invites us to share the comfort and assurance of the Gospel: Christ Jesus has earned full and complete forgiveness for all sins through His life, death, and resurrection.

While political activism is not a God-given mandate, Christians do have an obligation to work for the good of the state. Even our citizenship in a democracy obligates us to do just that. How we do it as Christians, though, varies from person to person as well as according to the issue and/or situation.

We ought not, for example, ask the country to force everyone to join a Christian church, for faith is a matter of the heart. Nor should we extend absolute forgiveness to all criminals and absolve them from punishment, even if they are repentant. Neither policy benefits the country.

When we participate in the private acts of politics (voting, for example), God's Word guides our decisions, but within the reality that our society truly is secular. And when speaking in public, we often will need to draw on natural law rather than God's Law.

Some public issues do not allow for a simple answer. Should homosexuality be considered mentally or emotionally unhealthy and be treated à la alcoholism? Should special laws prevent the discrimination against homosexuals in jobs or housing? Should same-sex "marriages" be recognized for tax and insurance purposes? As citizens, we recognize the need for every human to be treated fairly. We also recognize that homosexual lifestyles vary from the very discreet to open flaunting to aggressive proselytizing. When we are parents, our reactions vary according to whether children are involved in the situation or issue.

When no simple answers suggest themselves, the best we can do is to evaluate the issues carefully. Then we let our voices/votes be heard—and pray that the God of heaven and earth will continue to bless His creation in spite of our fallen nature. Without God's blessings, all creation would cease to exist.

At the same time, our decisions need to be made with some understanding of natural law—both its moral law as well as its "laws" about the way humans behave. Consider, for example, the question of homosexuals in the military. The question is not the morality of homosexuality any more than that of heterosexual fornication. Both are wrong, but who tries to keep fornicators out of the military? Nor is the question whether homosexuals as individuals have the ability or the patriotism necessary for service. Some have and do serve nobly. From my standpoint as a citizen in need of a quality military (and knowing that others may disagree with me), the question is whether allowing homosexuals to be open about their sexual orientation best serves the functional interest of the military.

Given the facts that (1) the vast majority of people agree with the natural law against homosexuality and that (2) a significant majority of service personnel are anything but tolerant of homosexual behavior, I do not believe sexual orientation should be an open issue for the military. The psycho-social implications are enormous. The military is not a social experiment. Again, others will disagree with this view; I use it as an example of how we as Christian citizens can make and press for decisions apart from forcing our theology on others.

Another example: Should homosexuality be accorded special rights/privileges in the manner of those given to minorities based on age, gender, and race? In this issue too, my conclusions might not be yours, but we all need to make decisions based on what will be good for our society. Aware of that, I know that some homosexuals have suffered unfairly in situations where sexual orientation should make no difference or create interpersonal conflicts. This ought not to be. I also know that antihomosexual attitudes will not be changed because of any laws and that, therefore, homosexuals will continue to suffer unfairly at times.

Finally, though, I believe that most cases of unfair discrimination against homosexuals can be handled through existing laws that do not afford them special rights as a minority. I stagger to think of the possible ramifications if new, wide-reaching laws were adopted. Could a *hetero*sexual fired from a job suddenly claim protection because he or she now claims to be a "closet *homo*sexual"? Could a person gain preferential treatment (as in some cases of racial discrimination cases) by claiming homosexuality—whether true or not? Will employers be required to hire homosexuals on the basis of their proportion of the population—and hire them for positions in which homosexuals will glorify their lifestyle? Because of these concerns, I believe society is best served if existing laws are enforced to combat unfair discrimination. I do not think that broad, sweeping new laws based on minority status should be enacted.

To summarize: The Christian response in the public arena to issues of homosexuality need not be unique to Christianity, nor need it be unanimous. We who hear God's Word know what He has said about a long list of sins. As citizens, we are called on to help decide how to structure our society for the good of all. For this, we ask God's blessing, even when we in the church differ from one another.

For Discussion

1. What should be the role of a Christian in society? Why?

2. How is God's Word the only completely trustworthy source of information concerning God's desire for all people?

3. How would you respond to the five statements regarding homosexuality found earlier in this chapter? Why?

4. Describe the tightrope we often walk as Christians—condemning sin while loving sinners. What do we risk if we lean to one side while ignoring the other? Why is balance so important for the Christian?

5. Discuss the author's arguments in "The Christian Response in the Public Arena" section. Do you agree or disagree? Why? Why is it so important to ask, "What would God have us do" as we make decisions?

6

Responding to the Individual Homosexual

Although dealing with homosexuality on the level of public policy is important, the crucial exchange for us as Christians occurs on the individual, personal level, one-to-one. But what to say? I doubt this book has answered all your questions; in fact, it may have raised new ones. That's okay. Be comfortable knowing that you don't have all the answers. Recognition of that lack is part of every growth process. At the same time, I hope you have the desire to continue to understand more about the person who struggles with homosexual desires and feelings. As you grow, I encourage you to maintain a balance between having a loving and open attitude and having the inner strength to hold to what Scripture teaches.

Also, be aware that you as a person can do nothing to make another person change; you can't just say the "right thing" and expect that your words will bring about repentance for righteousness. Only the Holy Spirit can do that. The only change over which you have control is within yourself. How will you react to the information that this person is a homosexual? How will this knowledge affect your relationship? I pray that the Holy Spirit will lead you to build up one another in Christ Jesus.

Some of what you say and do will vary, depending on whether the homosexual person who opens up to you is a friend or a relative and whether you are a pastor or lay leader who represents the organization called "church." I'll comment on those differences later in the chapter. The basics, however, remain, no matter what the situation. Only God truly changes hearts, and His Law and Gospel need to touch hearts on an individual basis. Stating the truth in love is difficult, especially if you know that it will at first offend the hearer. At the same time, we are called to speak the things we have seen and heard and know to be true.

I am not suggesting that you rush out to find the nearest homosexual and rain down God's wrath upon him or her. There is a time to speak, even to speak the Law, but that time usually comes *after* a time to listen. In the previous chapter, I mentioned that one of the first steps toward change is a crisis. Until a homosexual not only feels the pain and shame of the orientation and behavior but also faces some crisis, the motivation for change will not be present.

Listen with Acceptance

Your first step, therefore, has to be listening with an acceptance of the homosexual as one who has been both created and redeemed by Christ. Yes, there is sin, but sin exists in all of us. Acceptance of a person as a creation of God does not mean condoning or blessing that person's sin. Christian care does not give permission for what God forbids. It does mean that through your acceptance and care of the other as a person, you are building a relationship so strong and trusting that he or she knows it can survive should the homosexuality be revealed.

Acceptance may well be the greatest need homosexuals have. Their loneliness drives them to each other, and the care they receive from fellow sufferers feeds their misbelief that no one in the "straight world" cares about them enough to deal with the truth.

Keep the Knowledge Confidential

As part of that acceptance, assure the person that what has been shared will be kept confidential. He or she has opened to you some deep and shameful things, causing the person to be extremely vulnerable. Betraying the confidence shouts loudly that not only do you *not* accept the person but that you want others also to condemn him or her.

Sort Out Your Own Feelings/Reactions

Before going too far into the conversation, you will need to take a moment to evaluate your own feelings. As a Christian confidant, you may feel the other person's pain, but you need to be aware of your own feelings also. Is there a private reason you regret the person's choices? Are you personally saddened or hurt? Is the revelation so painful to you that you need time to reflect before the sharing resumes? If so, arrange for a specific time to continue the conversation. In order to help the person deal with the guilt and shame of homosexuality, you need to be able to focus on his or her problem rather than on a problem you might have listening.

Use Questions to Foster Openness

As the conversation continues, do not be afraid to ask questions. Rather than focus on specific deeds, ask questions that encourage the person to share his or her "story." Questions might include "When did you first notice these strange feelings?"; "How did you handle them at first?"; "Tell me about your past struggles"; or "What led you to open up now?" The importance of such openings are twofold. First, they encourage him or her (1) to self-reflect, (2) to organize thoughts and feelings about the problem, and (3) to put the problem as well as thoughts and feelings out in the light where they can be dealt with. Second, they show your genuine concern for and acceptance of the person.

Share God's Word

When you finally have the chance as a trusted friend to say that homosexuality is not within God's plan, do not expect immediate agreement. That might happen, depending on the level of shame the person has felt for years. More likely, though, the response will be defensive at first. "I'm gay and proud of it. If you have a problem with it, then you're 'homophobic' and you better get used to it!" These are harsh, defiant, and hurtful words. It's hard to listen to this without becoming very closed to the person and wanting to fire back. Instead of just firing back with "But it's wrong," a response such as "Why do you think that?" will at least give the opportunity for more communication.

Or the person may say, "I'm gay, and there is no other choice for me. I've tried to change, but I just can't seem to." A truthful and loving response might be, "It must be a very difficult struggle. God does love you even in the midst of what you may feel as very sinful and shameful. God does forgive, and I know that there is hope for real change." The answer holds to the very truths of both God's Law and His grace.

Consider the example of Jesus' gentle yet truthful confrontation when He interacted with the woman at the well in Samaria (John 4:1–42). He approached her, listened to her, and spoke truth gently without rejecting her as a person. The account powerfully illustrates how Jesus' love and grace were poured into her as her sin was exposed and she was enabled to believe in Jesus as her Savior.

At the same time, be prepared for rejection of your words. The crisis may not be important enough or the pain deep enough for the homosexual to be convicted of his or her sin. In that case, no matter how loving a response you give, little could be said to affect the person's heart. If there is no repentance, do not offer God's Gospel and grace, for they surely will be misapplied or trampled down. At the same time, I believe that God's offer of forgiveness needs to be spoken at the same time the Law is articulated. Since no one can fully know the heart of another, you don't know if the Law by itself may cause the hearer to despair so much that the Gospel will never be sought. That's why I suggest that as soon as the Law is spoken, the hearer be told of God's offer of grace and forgiveness in Christ for those who repent. If, however, the listener outright ridicules or rejects God's Law, the Gospel should not at that time be spoken.

Will you always know exactly the perfect words to say? No. But I am convinced that as you ask for the Lord's help and discernment from the Holy Spirit, He will help you grow in understanding and compassion for those in need. May the Lord bless your care.

Suggestions for Relatives

When it comes to family relationships, homosexuality is perhaps the most difficult issue. How do we show care and love without condoning the lifestyle? Can we accept our son or daughter, sister or brother, in spite of this? How will family gatherings be handled, especially if he or she asks to bring along the same-sex partner and expects the rest of the family to treat them as a "couple"? What boundaries will be set? Will the "rules" for family gatherings be different from private visits? Although not a specific topic of this book, you need to anticipate also how you will react and what you will do if and when your homosexual relative becomes HIV-positive or infected with AIDS.

Scripture does not speak directly to these matters. Yes, homosexuality is wrong. The question, however, is, how might you continue to speak the truth in love so that the hearer does not turn a deaf ear to you? How might you continue to show love to this family member the same way God does: even while we were yet sinners? Sometimes, what you do comes down to what you can tolerate in relationship. You may want to consult a pastor or counselor to help you work through this—without, of course, breaking any confidences.

In general, though, using the guidelines given above (listening, acceptance, nonthreatening questions, and speaking God's Law and Gospel) will be helpful.

Suggestions for Church Workers and Leaders

Your situation is unique, for you not only represent Christ to the homosexual, you also represent the stance of the church. Therefore, you will need to listen carefully in order to say the correct and appropriate words of Law and Gospel at the right time.

As a general rule, assume that the person who shares his or her homosexuality with you already knows and feels the brunt of God's Law. More than likely, that's why the person chose to open up to you. If the guilt is not verbalized, ask questions that allow confession. "How do you feel about your orientation and behavior?"; "What has your struggle been like for you?"; "Why did you choose to open up here?"

Knowing that the church and Scripture speak clearly about the sin, the homosexual had to summon up great courage and strength in order to share with you. Do not cut off communication by quoting unnecessary Bible verses of Law. If the person acknowledges sin and guilt, communicate the Gospel in word and action—and attitude. One of the best ways for the latter is to listen to and affirm the person as someone for whom you and God still love and care.

At the same time, do not expect an immediate and complete change by the person. Like most serious problems, homosexuality is deep-seated and part of a complex personality. The process of change includes lapses back into old patterns and sins. The crucial factor is whether one is repentant and desirous of healing and maintaining sexual integrity. If so, he or she needs all the love, grace, and acceptance that can be given in the name of Jesus.

It may seem too obvious to say, but the person who reveals homosexuality should be encouraged to continue (or begin) attending worship services. Everyone there is a sinner and in need of God's strength and forgiveness.

There may also be questions concerning whether or not the person should be permitted to partake of the Lord's Supper. Pastors responsible for that decision need to listen closely to the person. Private of individual confession and absolution is a most appropriate arena in which to deal with the questions of sin and faith and forgiveness. If he or she confesses the sin and asks for God's forgiveness and strength to amend life, the person should be admitted to Holy Communion—even encouraged to attend. But we cannot require a guarantee that the Spirit-wrought turnaround in the person's life is now totally complete. If it were required, no one could receive the Sacrament. Rather, as sinners who trust in Jesus, we long for and seek His forgiveness for the past as well as strength for the future.

If, however, the person is saying in reality that he or she simply wants to be accepted as is and blessed in a homosexual relationship, admittance to Holy Communion should be denied. I'm not suggesting that anyone can know the heart of another. Rather, we can only base the decision on what people say about themselves. Those who choose not to repent or recognize their need for forgiveness and grace are at the same time rejecting the value of Holy Communion. Withholding admittance is part of the way God intends for the church to deal with any sin. What may appear punitive and harsh is in reality an act of love and concern, for it points out the severity of unrepented sin and ultimately can lead a person back to Christ.

This was one of the most difficult things for me to grasp. As long as I did not acknowledge my sin, I continued to harbor feelings of shame and unforgiveness. The grace and love of

God were not fully known and accepted—not because of the homosexual nature of my sin or because God's grace was not sufficient, but because I was too afraid and too ashamed to open up and be vulnerable. Not until I let other people into the deepest level of my soul did I truly hear, believe, and receive God's forgiveness and healing.

God's grace is not accepted when we refuse to admit our need. When human sin is rationalized or justified as human weakness or as part of being human, there is no place for God's grace. It grieves me when people refuse to receive God's forgiveness by not recognizing their need. What great loss to turn away from God's everflowing and overflowing grace!

Jesus told the woman at the well in Samaria that "whoever drinks the water I give him will never thirst. Indeed, the water I give him will become in him a spring of water welling up to eternal life" (John 4:14). It was in the woman's acknowledgment of the truth of her sin that the living water began to flow within her. She was not to hide and keep her sin hidden. Jesus sought her out, found her shame, and did not condemn.

Many are still hiding. They believe that the things deep inside are so bad that no one could possibly know about them and still love the person. Such people are naked, ashamed, and afraid that God will call to them as He did to Adam and Eve: "Where are you?"

Where are you in your feelings about homosexuality? Where are you in any sin? The deepest and most shaming area of my life has been turned around to become the most traveled pathway of Jesus' entering my heart. That is His desire for everyone. May God bless your conversations of the heart.

For Discussion

1. Read John 4:1–42. How does Jesus' acceptance of the woman give hope to those who believe their sin is too great for God to forgive?

2. Describe Jesus' approach to the woman at the well. How might Jesus' approach with the woman be an appropriate approach for you as you seek to share God's Word with a homosexual?

3. Why is confession such an important and necessary step for healing?

4. Discuss some of the things you have learned by studying this course.

5. Write down other questions you may seek to have answered. Seek answers to these questions from the list of additional resources listed in this guide or from a trusted and informed professional.

NOTES

Chapter 2

1. Simon LeVay, "A Difference in Hypothalamic Structure Between Heterosexual and Homosexual Men" (*Science*, vol. 253, August 30, 1991), 1034–37.
2. J. Michael Bailey and Richard C. Pillard, "A Genetic Study of Male Sexual Orientation" (*Archives of General Psychiatry*, vol. 48, December 1991), 1089–96.
3. Joe Dallas, *Desires in Conflict: Answering the Struggle for Sexual Identity* (Eugene, OR: Harvest House Publishers, 1991), p. 92.
4. Joseph Nicolosi, *Reparative Therapy of Male Homosexuality: A New Clinical Approach* (Northvale, NJ; London: Jason Aronson Inc., 1991).
5. Elizabeth R. Moberly, *Homosexuality: A New Christian Ethic* (Cambridge: James Clark & Co., 1983), p. 2.

Chapter 3

1. Joe Dallas, *Desires in Conflict*, p. 282.
2. C. S. Lewis, as quoted in Wayne Martindale and Jerry Root, eds., *The Quotable Lewis* (Wheaton, IL: Tyndale House Publishers, Inc., 1989), p. 352.

Chapter 4

1. Exodus International is a worldwide coalition of Christian ministries that offer counsel and support to individuals coming out of lesbianism and homosexuality, as well as to their families, friends, and church leaders. As a connecting link between widely scattered ministries, Exodus seeks to provide support, communication, and resources of growth for these outreaches. Exodus also supports new ministries by offering resources to individuals or churches wishing to minister to homosexuals and lesbians. As a major part of their support work, an annual conference is organized and sponsored by Exodus. Contact information is located in the resources section at the end of the book.
2. Leanne Payne, *The Broken Image: Restoring Personal Wholeness through Healing Prayer* (Westchester, IL: Crossway Books, 1981), pp. 63–64.
3. Martin Luther, *Luther's Small Catechism with Explanation* (St. Louis: Concordia Publishing House, 1986), pp. 22–23.

Chapter 5

1. Bob Davies, "What the Bible Says about Homosexuality," (*Discipleship Journal,* issue 73, 1993), 26–30.

ADDITIONAL RESOURCES

Books

Comiskey, Andy. *Pursuing Sexual Wholeness.* Lake Mary, FL: Creation House, 1989.

Dallas, Joe. *Desires in Conflict: Answering the Struggle for Sexual Identity.* Eugene, OR: Harvest House Publishers, 1991.

Howard, Jeanette. *Out of Egypt: Leaving Lesbianism Behind.* Eastbourne, UK: Monarch, 1991.

Konrad, Jeff. *You Don't Have to Be Gay.* Hilo, HI: Pacific Publishing House, 1992.

Magnuson, Roger J. *Are Gay Rights Right? Making Sense of the Controversy.* Portland, OR: Multnomah, 1990.

Nicolosi, Joseph. *Reparative Therapy of Male Homosexuality: A New Clinical Approach.* Northvale, NJ: Jason Aronson Inc., 1991.

Payne, Leanne. *The Broken Image.* Westchester, IL: Crossway Books, 1981.

van den Aardweg, Gerard. *Homosexuality and Hope.* Ann Arbor: Servant Books, 1985.

Regeneration Books
P.O. Box 9830
Baltimore, MD 21284-9830

Ministry Contacts

Exodus International (Referral Network)
P.O. Box 2121
San Rafael, CA 94912
415/454-1017

Keys Ministries (Lutheran)
P.O. Box 97
Wykoff, MN 55990
507/352-4110